REALLY GOD?

A Guide to Bouncing Back when Life Has Thrown You Down

Orienthia Speakman

TYROPUBLISHING SERVICES

Really God?
A Guide to Bouncing Back When Life Has Thrown You Down

©2015 by Orienthia Speakman
Printed in the United States of America

ISBN 13: 978-0-9864385-30
ISBN 10: 0986438537

TYROPublishing Services
http://www.tyropublishing.com

Cover designed by: Stefani Miranda Graphics

All rights reserved. No part of this publication may be reproduced, distributed, or transmitted in any form or by any means, including photocopying, recording, or other electronic or mechanical methods, without the prior written permission of the author, except in the case of brief quotations embodied in critical reviews and certain other noncommercial uses permitted by copyright law. For permission requests, write to the author, addressed "Attention: Permissions Coordinator" in writing to the following address:

CR8NME Ministry
P. O. Box 1708
Pine Lake, Georgia 30072
http://www.pastoro.org
Contact: Pastor Orienthia Speakman

Printed in the United States of America

Dedication

To my *Father, the late Rev. Eddie Dorsey III*, I did it!! In our last sit down conversation you made me promise that I would one day become an author. You always encouraged me to become all that God has called for me to be and I so miss you not being here with me to actually see all of the things that have materialized. You were my father, my mentor, my best friend and I just wanted to make good on my words! I love you dad and this is just the start.

To my *Mom* thank you for your undying love and support as I continue to grow into this woman you have prayed for.

To my *children Alexcia and Creston*, you both have seen me go through some really hard times and I know sometimes you had to go through it with me, but NOT once did you ever complain. You both have been my strength and gave me great reasons to press forward even when I wanted to quit. I wanted and desired to be better in order to give you both an example of what RESILIENCE looks like so that you both can accomplish all that you set out to do in your lives. U both ROCK!!!

Thank you *ELITE6* for your confidence in me, your support and prayers.

Lastly, thanks to *everyone that spoke an encouraging word*, prayed for me and supported me as I LAUNCH OUT INTO THE DEEP!! Jacquis Coutee you sowed a seed in my life to write this before it was even begun. I had to say thank you.

Finally I would like to thank *the love of my life & my best friend*. Thank you for all of your sacrifices to help me with this project. Thank you for every time you listened to me frustrated and sometimes even fearful, but you always had love in your voice when you would say, "Orienthia you can do this, It is what you were created to do." I love you with everything in me and pray that God will keep our hearts knit together forever!!!"

God bless you all!!

Introduction

In 2007 the overwhelming feeling of shock and grief exploded in my body, because at this very time in my life I felt my whole world had come crashing down all around me. This was the year my mentor, my best friend, yes my father had died. And if this had not been detrimental enough, several months later my husband and I were kicked out of a church where we were leaders and had been serving for over five years and to top the year off, we were going through a divorce of enormous proportions after eight years of marriage. In fact, one day during this time, I can still recall vividly sitting alone on my living room floor, screaming (at the top of my lungs as loud as I could without choking) and crying streams of warm tears that simply dropped down my cheeks onto the floor leaving a small puddle. As I sat in my living room, one of my favorite rooms in the house, a room that used to bring me joy and a room that was once filled with laughter had in a twist of fate, become a room of mourning and sorrow and sadness. Feeling all alone with a sense of strange abandonment on one side, yet on the other feeling the presence of God; only a small still presence. At that moment of deep sorrow, I hung on to His presence as the tears kept flowing through my bloodshot eyes gazing specifically towards my ceiling and I let out a shout, "Really God!"; a shout that sent a wave through my body and throughout my home. That shout should have been heard from miles away, and must have reached through dimensions into the Holy of Holies. Nevertheless, I heard nothing from God, but my own screams, and it seemed at that very moment, God had abandoned me.

Quietly I questioned myself, "How can all of this be happening to me?"

Then I questioned God, "Have I not done all you asked?? Where are you in the midst of this mess?"

"What have I done so wrong, that I deserve all of this at one time?"

Look, If you're honest with yourself, you have asked the same question or something very similar. Really God, I believe is a question that every Christian or every person at some point, at many points of their lifes we ask this question. We ask this question based on life's trials, tribulations, unexpected things that go on in our lives. Disappointment, discouragement, just different things that happen that cause us to ask that question, *"Really God, am I really going through this for the first time, the second time or the third time?"* As believers, it is possible we may have all asked this question to God at one time or another. Many of us may not be so eager to admit willingly that we have asked the question "Really God?" Or if the question is, "Is this happening to me again?"

Whatever form we ask it in I believe we are asking God many times in our lives based on what we're going through. "Why is this happening or am I really going through this?" I believe that God placed this book in my spirit simply because I am a woman. Once someone asked me to give them one word that best described me and the word that came to my mind was *resilient* and so I want to be able to give a gift back to the Body of Christ to let them know that resilience really can be a gift that God gives us. If we look over our lives we have been able to bounce back from some things that we've been counted out of; or in other words we have been able to bounce back from many situations that we would not have thought we were able to come out of on our own.

As you read this book, let me just be honest, it is not for everyone!

This book is for the person that feels like they are in a dark place in their life right now.

This book is for that person that feels like they are trapped in their situation and can't see their way out.

This book is for that person that feels like they have had enough, and are saying, "If one more thing happens, I'm going to lose it!"

This book is for that person that is holding on to the promise of God but just can't see how it will happen, yet!

This book is for that person that knows in their heart there has to be a way out but I just don't know how to get there!

This book is bound to inspire, motivate and help coach you out of your problem , through your process and into your promise.

For every setback, God has your BOUNCE BACK in mind.

Acknowledging My Father

Have you ever found yourself among a rubbish heap of impossibilities? Let me explain. In 2007 I found myself in a rubbish heap of impossibilities, because most of my life as a child, a young woman, a wife and a leader in God's church I had done all of the "right things to do," making every attempt known to man to stay out of certain situations and just live a life pleasing in God's sight. The bible reminds us in *Mark Chapter 8:23, "With God all things are possible to them that believe."* I am not being presumptuous, nor am I trying to be redundant when I ask you the following question. Have you ever found yourself on mountain size rubbish heap of impossibilities? You see, rubbish is just a cute way of saying, trash! Trash is described as articles that have been discarded by the user and no longer needed or effective in their lives. So as I sat on the living room floor, crying out..."Really God?" I felt for a short time, I had been discarded, forgotten and left alone on a trash heap. Now I trust you can vividly see my dilemma at the time, while I attempted to give you a visual picture of my own personal Ziklag situation that I experienced not too long ago. Yes me, even though this smile you see today, I experienced a chain of events that would set off in motion the strength you see in my smile today.

Let me take you back to a story that was shared with me, over and over and over again by my father. He was my mentor, my friend, he actually coached me in the ministry. He died in the same year I was going through a spiral of uneventful shockwaves, and passed away after experiencing His second major heart attack. My last words to him were, "I love you." I am so grateful to God those were my last words to a man that brought so much happiness in my life and having laid the foundation of who I am today.

Ironically, I was quite prepared for this chain of events before I actually went through them. Spending 5 years in a church and being asked to leave quietly. I was told to lie to the members about my exit in order to keep the church intact. I had been pulled on too much by the members, they were depending on my strength, talent, experience, knowledge and wisdom a bit too much and it seemed to have created dissension among the leaders…so very discreetly I was asked to move on. My dad must have known beforehand because he diligently prepared and trained me to be strong from the time before I was born.

God told Jeremiah, "Before I formed you in your mother's belly I knew you, before your were born I set you apart, I appointed you as a prophet to the nations." (Jeremiah Chapter 1:5)

My dad used to always remind me of…this is probably gonna sound weird but I'm gonna put it out there because I don't know if it has any relevance to my life. But my dad used to always tell me this particular story about when my Mom was pregnant how he thought…how *they* thought up until the time of me being born that I was a boy. And so when my mom gave birth to me my dad (it's hilarious) told them, *"look this is not my child because y'all told me that this was a boy from the time we did the ultrasound."*

And so throughout my life he would, on occasion, smile lovingly at me and say to me, *"You have the beauty of a woman but you have some personality traits that are so manly to the point you should have been a boy."*

In other words what I imagine he was trying to say to me was that my strength sometimes resembles that of a man in a sense of just knowing how to take things and deal with them because sometimes you know, as women we kind of get emotional. To some people, we (women) may be seen as fragile or weak.

But he was saying, *"You know when I look at you you're so beautiful on the outside but some of the ways you tackle things and you handle things you could have been a man."*

I don't know if that brings clarity, but when he passed it brought so much clarity to me because I could never understand during our talks, especially when I was much younger. I felt as if he was calling me a boy! I could not grasp seeing myself that way, as I understand today, he was speaking of my having a tough exterior and a soft interior. For example, spiritually speaking, he was talking about my ability to handle more of life than most women could handle at one time and still stand strong in the sense not staying in my feelings or being emotional.

Hearing this from him off and on, really helped me understand myself and how he saw me as I walked in the footsteps of his shadow. One example of my tough exterior, unfortunately had to rise up during our preparation to bury him. As the eldest daughter I had to take on all of the responsibility of making sure the funeral arrangements were completed as he would have desired and this was one of my most difficult challenges to date. Of course I leaned on my dad's siblings to help in many areas, but for the most part I held the bulk of responsibility.

As I mourned, I had to do what I had to do. This was one of those times when doing what is necessary overrides doing what you desire to do, because I had to push and press in order to get through this time. In the back of my mind...well my mind was numb, but the ounce of thinking I could pull up out of my being, were the thoughts of God's promise that He would never leave me alone. And this was one of the moments when I told God, as I sat in my living room, *"You might as well kill me now because I will never preach again." "You took the one thing from me that meant so much. I would have rather you..* (yes I did say this), *"take one of my children because I could have replaced them and left me my father."*

I leaned on my dad for wisdom, advice, problem solving, trouble shooting and the list goes on. I could bounce things off of him. I was just in love with my dad. We had a bond that was so tight on both an emotional and spiritual level that I cannot even comprehend until this date. I personally believe God gave me the type of Father that showed me what He (God) Himself is really trying to show to people. My dad had many of the same qualities as God has. My dad was so non-judgmental, he somehow noticed the good qualities in everyone who came into his company. My dad was so forgiving of people who had wronged him, even me at times. My dad was so stern in the times he needed to be stern. My dad mentored me in ministry and in my personal life. My dad would jack me up during the times when I needed to be put in check. My dad loved me, even when he had to show me tough love. My dad and for some reason even though he was here for only those 49 years, (which was not 49 for me because at this time I was only 33 years old), but of the years that God allowed him to be in my life…he just meant so much to me.

And often nowadays, I continue to hold on to the promise he made, that he was always going to be here. Even during the moments of writing my first book, I expected to share this moment with him. Even those moments of me going from just preaching at my little small church to God just opening doors all over. I cry often because I miss him so much. He was the person I could talk to about everything. He was my counselor and my coach. And because I could talk to him about everything, even now, I often will go to his grave site and just sit there. I do know he's not there, but it just gives me a peace that when I get really, really heavy with life and different things that go on I go and I just sit at his grave site and I just talk and I get a calming peace. Because I'm walking in things that he told me I would walk in but he's not here to see it. And sometimes that's just not you know, something I'm too happy about. But I have to move on and I have to go on in order to complete the vision that God has ultimately for my life. Anybody who meets me, they know about my dad Reverend Eddie Dorsey. They will know about him because I always talk about him. That's just how much he has meant to my spiritual walk and my day to day life. He was always there, and I will forever miss him and celebrate his life and fulfill his legacy.

Contents

Dedication		*3*
Introduction		*5*
Acknowledging My Father		*9*

Chapter I	Am I Really Here?	17
Chapter II	Assessing the Damage	23
Chapter III	Accepting My Pit Moment	32
Chapter IV	Finding My Mind-Shift	37
Chapter V	Resilience	44
Chapter VI	Process before the Promise	55
Chapter VII	Dead Garments	68
Chapter VIII	A Woman After God's Own Heart	79
Chapter IX	It's Time to Get My Life	86
Chapter X	Behind the Kodak Smile	94

Conclusion	*99*
Meet Pastor Orienthia Speakman	*101*

Recognizing where you really are is very vital to your moving forward from or out of any condition, Understanding your location is key to finding the correct path you should be on. Not necessarily your geographic location but In these opening scriptures of this text we see that David had come home and everything had been destroyed. David and his men had been sent home from battle,they are already tired from the travel only to come home to see their homes in smoke and in ruins and their families had been taken captive. At this time David's home was a place called Ziklag.

Chapter I

Am I Really Here?

I Samuel Chapter 30:1-6

*A*nd it came to pass, when David and his men were come to Ziklag on the third day, that the Amalekites had invaded the south, and Ziklag, and smitten Ziklag, and burned it with fire;

And had taken the women captives, that were therein: they slew not any, either great or small, but carried them away, and went on their way.

So David and his men came to the city, and, behold, it was burned with fire; and their wives, and their sons, and their daughters, were taken captives.

Then David and the people that were with him lifted up their voice and wept, until they had no more power to weep.

And David's two wives were taken captives, Ahinoam the Jezreelitess, and Abigail the wife of Nabal the Carmelite.

And David was greatly distressed; for the people spake of stoning him, because the soul of all the people was grieved, every man for his sons and for his *daughters: but David encouraged himself in the Lord his God.*

I wanna just start right here and say a prayer for everyone reading this book that has been poured out of my heart and soul by our Father, like a drink offering, poured out from my heart to yours.

And as the word says...David encouraged himself in the Lord. Father in the name of Jesus we come before you right now Lord giving you glory, honor and praise. I ask that Lord God that you will speak throughout the pages of this book, a word into the spirits of everyone who reads this and a word that will catch their souls ablaze. Lord God and cause them to be encouraged within themselves. Lord I thank you right now God that your anointing is present on these pages that can remove every burden and destroy every yoke of bondage. I thank You right now God that You are present and we feel Your presence. And I just thank You for what You're getting ready to do in our lives. And we thank You for it now in Jesus name. Amen.

My desire is to remind each of you right now that your attitude will always determine your outcome. In verse 6, David encouraged himself. Many of us are at a point where we're going through similar circumstances and situations in our lives. We're looking at circumstances that may not be lining up with what we think should be experiencing at this point in our lives. Some of what we may be experiencing may not feel so good and these experience have taken us off guard. Just when we thought we were on the road to success, an issue occurred that just seemed to knock us off of our spiritual feet. Yes those shoes are cute, and those heels were as high as we could possibly stand up in, but we got knocked back down to the lowest place in our lives.

Some of our battle scars were showing, but we were able to cover them up with a good Mac concealer; other wounds had just healed over and the scar had almost disappeared right before we reached our destination.

Many of us are facing some things we just don't have time for right now, and looking at some others (things) that we may not even wanna be bothered with right now. We are head on with some ugly place that to no fault of our own we have found ourselves in, but David learned how to encourage himself. When we start out in the beginning, verse 6 lets us know that David is coming back from a different place. He's coming back and coming home. He is in a good mood, tired and ready to relax from his long journey. He is ready to let his hair down so to speak, and ready to greet his family most likely with hopes of having a huge dinner ready on the table.

He's already on the run from Saul and when he gets home he sees that everything that he's built, everything that he's worked hard for, everything that he left behind has now been utterly destroyed. See, I don't know if y'all have ever been in that place. Where the very thing that you built up. The very thing that you worked so hard for. The very thing that you had an expectation to last forever; when you turn your back and you turn around that very thing is not standing. That very person is not there. That very situation is not making you feel the way that you thought it should make you feel. See I don't know about any of you but I've had some Ziklag moments in my life.

I've had some situations that caused me to wanna question God asking, "Where are you God, in my life?"

"Where are you and how are you working this situation out?"

"What is really going on in my life right now because things are not lining up the way Your word says they should line up?"

You see David had a moment in Ziklag. But see, it wasn't just David that was affected. He was not alone in this, all his men that were affected as well. Remember, many times when you are going through, the people that are the closest in your life are affected by some of the same circumstances you're having to go through as well. Now allow me to paint the picture, imagine David looking at their homes, burned down to the ground. David was looking at how their cattle might have been destroyed. Their cattle represented much of their income.

David must have been exasperated as he reminded God, *"Now God, I've been on this assignment per your instruction and I followed the plans you gave me."*

"Why is it when I come back my home is destroyed when I was doing what You were telling me to do?"

"I was being obedient to what You called me to do. I was doing the assignment that You had me on and God when I come back home to my own home I find my home destroyed."

"But not only is my home destroyed. My wife and my family have been taken captive. I don't know what's going on. I don't know if they've killed them."

"I don't know what's going on but the most precious things in my life have now been taken away."

Now stop and consider. What would you do if something similar happened to you? I understand some of you may be right in the middle of a mess at this very moment. Perhaps you were laid off of your job, was just diagnosed with a debilitating sickness, or even served papers from pending lawsuit against you. You know what I am saying? Can you see the picture I'm painting? The very thing that was meant to take you off balance and cause you lose your composure may be the very test sent by God. Just like David you were taking care of your business, doing the thing you were called to do; but instead of being rewarded, you found yourself under siege.

Many times the attack comes suddenly, you just don't have time to respond because you are caught off guard. Have you ever felt you had been personally violated, raided, overthrown or just knocked down for the count? Then if you have, you can see yourself on the same journey that David was on and even before the shock can wear off, it's time to take an assessment of casualties, with counting yourself as number one and examining the ones who are accompanying you and in addition those who are looking at you as their example of strength; but if the truth be told correctly, you really don't feel very strong in this condition you have found yourself in by the adversary called life.

Chapter II

Assessing the Damage

You see David had a moment in Ziklag, but David wasn't alone and he was not the only person who was affected. All of his men were also affected; they were with him in the midst of his test. Many times folks who like to celebrate with you, hang out with you and party with you are not all that excited when you are going through a rough situation. David's party was not an ordinary type of party, because God had called David to do an assignment that was dangerous, which he thought ended successfully because he overcame the enemy. But isn't it just like Satan to blindside you from the rear when you least expect him to? These same men who had fought like the soldiers David himself appointed for the task, found themselves in the middle of a critical situation they did not buy into. Can you lend me your spiritual ears for a moment? They must have had some cussing and fussing, murmuring and whispering, because not only was David's property destroyed and family taken hostage, but so was theirs. They all found themselves smack down in the middle of a hostile takeover.

Sometimes the people that are around you in your life are affected by some of the things you're having to go through as well. David was looking at their homes burned down. David was looking at how their cattle had been destroyed. Their homes represented their shelter and their cattle represented their ability to provide for their family's future. I can see David now with his head in his hands screaming, "God, I was on assignment for you!!! I followed your complete instructions. I initiated the plan, exactly the way you laid it out!"

With anguish David may have asked, "But why God?"

"Why is it when I return home; my home is destroyed when I was only doing what You told me to do?"

"I was being obedient to what You called me to do."

"I was doing the assignment that You had me on and God when I come back to my own home I find it destroyed. Not only is my home destroyed, my wife and my family have been taken captive."

"I don't know what's going on. I don't know if they killed them. I don't know what's going on but the very most precious things in my life have now been taken away."

At this very moment I can only imagine David weeping inside of his soul, with so many questions swimming around inside his mind. Feeling confused, perplexed and exhausted from his long journey.

But before he could really concentrate on his own misfortune, he had to have looked behind him and saw the faces of his men. Those faces looking back at him with a countenance of anger, confusion, and fear staring right back at him.

The Bible says that David was very distressed. David was very disappointed. David was very hurt. But when I looked at the scripture I noticed the words written down state, *"all the men and all the people were distressed."* But then it goes on to say, *"They were so distressed that they started turning on David."*

So now the people that you think are in this thing with you. The people that you have prayed for. The people that you have served. The very people that you have worked hand in hand with now all of the sudden are in their little corner talking about how they're getting ready to stone you. See, as believers we have to realize that sometimes we get blamed for circumstances that we had no control over. Because we are the pivotal point person in the situation we find ourselves on the brink of being stoned by the very people we have served, because we are the leader and they hold us accountable for everything. Go ahead and enjoy the times of victory, shout during the times of celebration but when disappointment rears it's ugly head be prepared to deal with offense.

Listen, David was the leader, and now the people are looking at David like this is all his fault. The thoughts they were thinking may not have come across their lips, but could possibly be located in their mind.

"If we had not been with you, our wives would not have been taken. If we had not been with you our homes would still be standing."

"If we had not been with you, our finances would be where they need to be."

"If I had not been with you, I would be prospering in a total different direction in my life."

"If I had not been connected with you, things would be working better in my life."

And now they're talking about stoning the very person that they called their leader. David has found himself in a hard place. Because not only did he lose everything like they did, but now the very people that should be standing with him have now turned their back on him as if they never knew him at all. The same people whom you prayed for, helped get their child out of jail, and led to Christ may turn away from you when things begin to get tough, just like David, you may find people can be quite fickle.

"If I was…" When I was looking at this situation I started looking at myself, my own life. And although at this very moment as I write, my desire is to walk you over to verse seven, but I can't just yet. Do you recall in verse 7, David asks for the priest? I don't wanna even jump down to verse 7 yet because I would rather hang out right here in verse 6.

And David was greatly distressed; for the people spoke of stoning him, because the soul of all the people was grieved, every man for his sons and for his daughters: but David encouraged himself in the LORD his God. (2 Samuel Chapter 30:6)

Assessing the Damage | 27

The people were grieved because this loss seemed to much to bear, too harsh to deal with and just too abrasive for the mind to comprehend. The Bible says the people were *greatly distressed*[1]. You see, to be distressed is one thing, but to be greatly distressed takes the dynamics presented to us in the text to an entirely different paradigm. In this scripture, distressed is an adjective and is described as experiencing anxiety, sorrow, or pain. *Greatly*[2] is placed strategically before the word *distressed* and it's meaning is *to a great extent or degree.* Therefore to be greatly distressed is far worst than being distressed alone would you agree? The people were greatly distressed and when someone is so distraught it is fair to assume they are not thinking straight, and it is also possible they may have crossed over to a state of rage. They were at the point of "discussing" or even contemplating stoning David at this point and in spite of all the people had gone through with him and for him, they had obviously reached a boiling point of no return.

But remember, we know David was a leader, and we also know this David as King, so trust me when I tell you this was not his first time operating in heated atmospheric pressure. *The Bible says that David encouraged himself.* It didn't say that David went and

---

1 "Distressed - Merriam-Webster." 2006. 21 Apr. 2015 <http://www.merriam-webster.com/dictionary/distressed>

2 "Greatly - Merriam-Webster." 2005. 21 Apr. 2015 <http://www.merriam-webster.com/dictionary/greatly>

sought the priest at that moment of decision. Many times when we are in the valley of decision we call our best friend or a family member for advice. As I take a small peek over there in verse 7, this is not the time to change lanes, because there is a lesson to be caught right there in verse 6. Remember, David was the odd man out, a mob was staring him down, and he had a hit on his life. But instead of David calling on his help, he did something so peculiar and so out of the ordinary.

Instead of taking the opportunity to go running scared, the word says that David encouraged himself. Before he even went to the tabernacle. Before he even called for the priest. Before he even laid his head down to pray. The Bible says that David encouraged himself.

Now when I started looking at that scripture closely I thought to myself; he didn't call anybody and he didn't immediately go to the house of the Lord. Actually, it had to be something that David had on the inside of him and all that was already locked on the inside of him to be able to pull on during his time of need. You see, many times the problem with us is that we are looking for people to hold our hand throughout the duration of our situation.

We often look for people to pat us on the back and yell out, *"Go ahead on boo, you got this!"*

There is someone reading this and you are looking for people to hold your hand. You are looking for the pastor to pray over you and pray you out of your situation. But I wrote this book to let you

Assessing the Damage | 29

know personally from me, the Bible says that *David encouraged himself.* Let's examine this situation a bit closer, because I hear you in the spirit realm saying, "How can a man in that situation, stop and encourage himself?" Many of you reading this may not have had your Ziklag experience yet, but let me help you out right this moment and explain this place that many people like you and me have already discovered, called Ziklag. *This place is a natural location and it is also a spiritual point of reference..*

When God gives each of us our natural talents, spiritual gifts, callings and then place us on various assignments in the Kingdom, there is a great chance you will have to end up in a place called Ziklag. Ziklag is the Biblical name of a town that was located in the Negev region in the south of what was the Kingdom of Judah.[3,4] This was also the residence and private property of David. Smith's Bible Dictionary defines Ziklag's meaning as *"winding"*.[5] Winding can have a similar meaning as binding, to be wrapped, coiled, or wound[6]. It could have also denoted the journey that it took to get there along a long winding road. But however you describe this place, David was in

---

[3] "Ziklag - Free definitions by Babylon." 2006. 22 Apr. 2015 <http://www.babylon.com/definition/Ziklag/>

[4] "Ziklag - Free definitions by Babylon." 2006. 22 Apr. 2015 <http://www.babylon.com/definition/Ziklag/>

[5] "Ziklag - Meaning of Ziklag in Smiths Bible Dictionary (Bible ..." 2005. 22 Apr. 2015 <http://www.bible-history.com/smiths/Z/Ziklag/>

[6] "Wound up | Define Wound up at Dictionary.com." 2007. 22 Apr. 2015 <http://dictionary.reference.com/browse/wound+up>

the middle of a mess, but he made the decision and shifted the dynamics in his own favor and begin to encourage himself. David did not place the focus on the crowd, nor did he pass the blame on anyone else. David did what real leaders do, he looked beyond his location.

Let's go a bit deeper. *Ziklag is a place, and a position; an unexpected place; a place of discouragement; a place of depression; a lonely place; a place of where you feel like you may have lost everything; a place where God seems far, far away.*

And one of the things that I like about this particular story is that many of us have at one point in our lives have felt like we have either lost everything, or have felt like something or someone has been taken from us.

We've felt like maybe we have lost a loved one. Maybe we have lost a job. Maybe we have lost a good relationship with our children. Maybe we have lost a marriage.

And sometimes when you have too many bad experiences coming towards you at one time, you may feel like you are at a place of depletion. I look to my own personal life, as I shared with you earlier. In the same year, I went through a humiliating divorce, I experienced my father passing and if that had not been enough, I was also asked to leave my church where I had been Co-Pastor for 5 years. It was in this place, my personal Ziklag, where I sat alone in a state where it seemed like everything that meant something to me was gone...was lost.

And that's a deep situation to be in. *I felt physically tired. I felt mentally tired. I felt like I was unable to breathe. I could not breathe. I was gasping for air but I just could not resuscitate myself, by myself.*

Now since I have been there, I can relate to how David felt when he first returned home. First of all let me remind you again, remember, he had just come off an assignment orchestrated by God. I can relate to that scene, as if I was there with David looking on as a witness taking notes. This happened in slow motion, so I kept being in that place where I felt like I came off of an assignment that God had asked me to go on.

God asked me to go here and preach. I went and preached. I went and prayed. I went and did everything that I felt that God was asking me to do and then I come home. My house is all torn up. My marriage is now ended. My father has now died and now the place that I was going to on a consistent basis that I thought was a place of peace, that I would go and assist God's people in their spiritual growth, I was being asked to leave.

So yes, I felt like I was in a place of Ziklag. Now before I really could not personally identify with that because it is those circumstances where you go to the doctor and he says, "you have cancer." Or you go to your job that you were employed over 30 years and they're giving you a pink slip and letting you go. These are the kinds of situations that can easily take the breath out of you. You feel like you are the only one "going through," as if someone dropped you down into a deep hole and left you there all alone.

Chapter III

Accepting My Pit Moment

Have you ever driven down the side of a winding hill where you seem to be on the edge and all you can see is a huge drop on each side with no where to turn around and your only choice is to keep going forward, spiraling downward? Once you get to the bottom into your valley experience, only looking up to discover you are now down deep into a pit. From Ziklag to the pit experience can be an unforgettable experience that no one can relate to unless they too have been there.

So while I was deep in my pit, coming to from the pure shock of it all was when I began asking God questions. I said, *"God can you show me how David encouraged himself?"*

"Can you tell me how he did this because many of us are looking to go to a specific place."

"We are looking for particular people to fix our life."

Accepting My Pit Moment | 33

"We are looking for particular things to get us out of our situation."

But David only had himself. Then I had to think on this situation in my mind. This is the same little shepherd boy that used to tend to the sheep in the field. He is the same young boy that had to kill the lion and the bear at some place in time and these are the same points of reference that caused him to realize that he could also slay the giant Goliath. David had to go back and remember all the victories that God had already given him in every situation all throughout his life. Because when he was at the end of his rope, God showed up in his life each and every time.

Of course, David had the strength and the memory of past experiences he had faced, to encourage himself. Reminder, we are still in verse 6, and this scripture starts out telling you that David was distressed but by the end of verse 6 David has now gone from being greatly distressed to encouraged! In this one placement of text, David went from being distressed to a place of encouragement.

In the middle of your own personal pit experience you have got to understand that sometimes you must look back and pull on some of the things that God has brought you through. When the doctor told you that you might not make it. You got to pull from your repertoire of experiences. You think God brought me out of that. When you've lost your job and now God has given you two jobs you gotta go back and pull that out of your repertoire. You say God I made it through that. When God gave you peace when the man left you or the woman left you you gotta go back and pull your repertoire. Maybe you have lost everything but with God you have recovered it all! Right in the middle of your pit you have found yourself in, you really don't have to pull on no one else's testimony. You've got to learn to pull on what God has brought you out of. I can share my testimony with you, but at the end of the day, you are the only one who knows what God has brought you out of.

Only you know what tests that God has brought you through.

Only you know what God has pulled you out of when you couldn't talk to nobody. When you didn't have anybody else there with you. Only you know that in your darkest moment that God stepped into your situation.

I decree and declare, if He brought you out of that, He is going to bring you out of this! Like David, we have to create a power-shift in our own minds. Like David, we have to proclaim, "M*y circumstance don't dictate my out come!*"

Just say to yourself right now while you are in the pit, *"I might be sitting in this situation right now but God, You are going to bring me out!"*

When I was in my pit, I knew God was faithful because I had already experienced situations from my past. As I stated earlier, while I was down deep in my pit, I could not breathe. I could hardly gasp for air. I had gone down so low, so deep and it seemed so dark. But while I was right there I remembered some things that for a short minute I had forgotten. As I sat there, I begin to remind God by crying out to Him saying, *"God You can bring a fresh breath back in my life."*

As I wept through my soaked blanket, I went on to remind him, *"God I know that You didn't leave me here to die, but You did leave me hanging. Lord but I do remember what You did for me before, and I know you are able to deliver me again."*

Saints love to quote this thing, *"Lord when I think of the goodness of God and all that He's done for me my soul cries hallelujah!"* But, there are times you have to go back and have what I call, *a thinking moment*. A *thinking moment* is when we have to go way back in our past and think about how God brought us out of similar situations. These situations are God's tests and trials that we had to endure, because God wanted them to to be recordings in our mind about how he brought us out once before and we needed a point of reference to understand, He can and will do it again! Hallejuah!

David had to encourage himself because there was nobody around him who was trying to help him, instead those around him were plotting to kill him. The people around him were concentrating on their own situations and they had tunnel vision. They could not see past their own problems, they couldn't even see God right there in the middle of their mess.

Let me remind you there is not a lot of room in the pit. The pit can be a lonely place. David's men were in the pit with him. They were looking for somebody to blame in this terrible situation. David could have done the same. He could have blamed God for being in that situation. Isn't it ironic in the middle of your pit, God will remind you of your promise? David had a promise that was made to him. He was promised that he was going to be king. But see in the middle of your pit you must remind God of your promise. In the middle of your pit you must hold on to your promise. God has promised something to you but while you are waiting on your promise to manifest, you can still be stuck, deep down, inside of a dark pit simply in search of a way out!

Chapter IV

Finding My Mind-Shift

One important point that I noticed in verse 6 is the Bible didn't say that David went directly to God while he was in this solemn state of discouragement, dismay, and depression. In addition, the Bible didn't allude to the fact that David turned to any of his friends or called any of his friends to a prayer meeting. The bible explicitly says that, *"David began to encourage himself."* When the bible said that, I believe David began to reflect on some of the things that God had brought him out of in order to encourage him. He may have thought, *this may be a very low, low state but if God brought me out of the lion, the bear and all of those situations where I almost died but (as a shepherd boy) I was able to gain the victory. God brought me out of the situation where I was facing a 12 foot giant Goliath with nothing but 5 smooth stones and He brought me out of that!* Sometimes we have to take our mindset back to all of the victories that God had previously given us in order to push us and shift our minds to a place of positivity instead of negativity.

Most of us are experiencing different situations and some of us may have encountered the same types of issues. For some of us they seem quite difficult, but if you go back and recall, there are different situations in your life that you did make it through having no idea how you might make it out, but you did! As I remind you to shift your attitude or shift your mindset, I'm explaining the example that David demonstrated and have come to a realization moving forward that I have got to go inward for my encouragement instead of searching outward.

My Ziklag place involved a series of major events that took place simultaneously in one year. My marriage ended, the event of losing my father, and being kicked out of the church I attended, there were many amazing victories that occurred previously that I could pull from the inside of me. These past places would remind me that I am more than a conqueror! They reminded me that God is still with me! They also reminded me that although I didn't think I was gonna make it out of that, God had a track record with me, and if He was able to do it back then, He can bring me out of this too.

On the way out of his pit experience David had to shift in his own mind. He had to make the determination that even though my situation is negative I'm going to remain positive. Yes, my situation may look like this now, but I know that this is not the end of the road for me. *Everything around me may be breaking down and breaking loose, but I know that what I'm seeing is only temporary.*

So you gotta start speaking to your situation and proclaiming with authority, *you are only temporary!* You have got to tell your situation, *you're not going dictate how I feel! You are not gonna dictate what I think! You are not going to dictate what I am!* If you don't actually speak to your current situation, you will allow those negative things to remain and negative thoughts to enter into your mind. Negative thoughts become negative words and negative words become negative actions. And you will keep spiraling in a whirlwind of negativity.

Besides, David said, *"I'm not gonna remain here is this place of negativity in the company of negative people, in spite of what I am going through at the present, I'm going remain positive. Not because I am the greatest but because I serve the greatest. Not because of who I am. Not because of anything I've done. I've gotta hold on to this promise because I know the One who made me the promise."* See, if God said He's gonna do it He's not like man that He should lie. He's not like man that He should repent. If God's word says it, then you hold on to the promise. If God's word acknowledged it, then it is coming to pass. Come hell or high water, it will come to pass. David made a resolve that his current situation would not be dictated by the people around him. David decided that he was going to remain positive right in the state he was in.

The last part of the story went like this. Amazingly, David was able to recover all things and not just the things that he had but he gained much more. What this means to you and me is we have got to learn although we are in a negative situation but if we begin to act positive while in our negative situation not only will we recover that which was lost, we will recover more than what we had when we started. David had to strengthen himself. He couldn't look around at everybody else because there wasn't anyone around for him to for him to look to. David had to look within. But guess what? In order for you to be able to look within you must have the word of God already planted inside of you.

You also have a part to play in all of this. Because as Christians we often get lazy. *You want Jesus will fix it for you because He know just what to do. But in return, Jesus is saying you ought to know just what to do too... because I am waiting on you.* We wanna sit back and wait on God when God is waiting on us too. Heaven is looking at you saying what are not you gonna do? Because you know this is an open book test right? You know that before you go through the test that the teacher has already given you what you need to go through the test. Every time you go through something God has already given you what you need in order to be able to access throughout the process of what you're dealing with. But you know what we do? We allow the enemy to talk to us. Then we allow the enemy to give us his thoughts and we start sounding negative like him. We begin speaking about our situation and we start becoming negative with our actions. And then we're all wrapped up in all that stuff.

On the contrary, if we would simply remain focused and keep our thoughts positive. Allow me to explain, when I say the words *stay positive* I'm not talking about speaking those positive affirmations that you got off *Dr. Phil* or *The Oprah Winfrey Show*. This is not an attempt to bash either of them, but my intentions are set a bit higher than those so-called positive affirmations. Basically, I am talking about being positive in the word of God. I am expressing the importance of reading scriptures from the Holy Bible and saying you know what God said in his word. That is what I am discussing here about positivity and having a positive flow.

Again, back to verse 6, David made the key decision declaring in his own mind, *"I'm not wasting my time by looking at what's going on around me. I'm not wasting my thoughts thinking about what the people are saying about me. I'm not even gonna waste my breath explaining how we ended up here. I'm only going to look within myself. I've got to dig deep on the inside of me and pull out what I have on the inside of me. I've got to take myself back in remembrance of what God has already done. I have to make the positive decision that this thing is gonna shift and this thing is gonna change. I gotta make the decision that my circumstance may be negative but I don't have to be negative in my circumstance."*

Answer these questions below and I trust you will discover a positive outcome in every situation you face in your future.

Did you know that you can be positive in a negative situation?

Did you know that you don't have to allow your situations to dictate what your outcome is?

Did you know that God has already said that you have the victory and therefore you should walk like you have the victory at all times?

Did you know that sometimes you may not be able to get to the pastor or you might not be able to get to the elder so you've got to be able to have your own personal arsenal to be able to deal with your current situations?

Did you know that some of your situations stay long because you invited them to have a seat in your life instead of escorting them right on out the door?

Did you know that you define a lot of the stuff in your life by your negative thinking and your negative talk?

Did you know that some of the stuff that you're dealing with right now you brought it on yourself?

Did you know that the devil only has as much power in your life as you give him access to?

Did you know that you have access to two teams every time you open up your mouth? Either angels are working or the devil and his demons are working depending on what's coming out of your mouth.

Did you know that all your circumstances have you as a center block on the inside of them so therefore you have got to look at you to see how most of this stuff is starting?

Saints you know some of us love to say that *the devil made me do it.* We love to say that *the devil is attacking me.* But you've got to look at you. You have got to look at what clothes you are wearing. You have got to look at what coat you are wearing and recognizing in the moment *this is where I am, now what am I going to do about myself and for myself.*

Now take a long look at you, accessing the damage and accepting that you are really here and moving forward. Because I believe that simply moving out of something is not really making a determination but when we get in pursuit of something that's a little bit more driven than just feeling like *I gotta get out of this. Feeling like you have to get out is basically depending on your own strength, making a determination that you will get out of this, is depending on your faith in God and your power to actually move forward.*

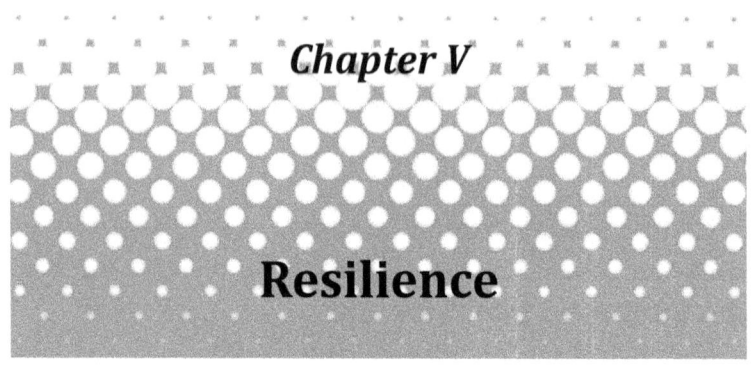

Chapter V

Resilience

Really God is a subtle question many Christians or possibly every person at some point in their life has asked. We ask this question based on life's trial, tribulations, unexpected things that go on in our lives. Disappointment, discouragement, just different paths we cross, detours, or distractions that attempt to take us off course and cause more delay. "Really God?" is likened to a big sigh of disbelief or even anguish that causes us to ask that question. "Really God?" is often asked from the standpoint of fear so intense that you find yourself asking a question you already know... like God...the answer to. Jesus will work it out, rings true in your ears, but instead of resting in the facts of God's faithfulness, we tend to do the opposite, asking the question... "Really God?" I believe the words just slip out, sometimes by accident, as we ask God the questions spinning around in our heads. We tend to lose focus on Him and although we may have experienced it before, well you know what I am about to say already, right? We act all brand new, but this thing hurts like a ton of bricks hit us and has us pinned down to the ground with no one around to help us.

Hey God! Are you there we ask at the sound of a whisper through our tears.

Can you hear me? Do you see what I'm going through?

How could you let this happen to me again?

I believe that God placed this in my spirit simply because I am a woman or...someone asked me once to give them one word that would describe me and the word that came to me was *resilient* and so I want to be able to give a gift back to the body of Christ to let them know that resilience really can be a gift that God gives us.

But first, allow me to share the following excerpt from Dr. Barbara Fredrickson a psychologist and researcher with you. I don't usually throw my education around but I do have a degree in psychology and I want to share something highly important that I often refer to with you. *Dr. Barbara Fredrickson* in her book, *Power of Positivity* has written that positive emotions are very important for resiliency.[7] Now you have got to understand that *resiliency* is the ability to recover from misfortune. It means to be capable of withstanding the shock without permanent deformation to your situation. Simplified, *resiliency*

7"Positivity: Top-Notch Research Reveals the Upward Spiral ..." 2015. 22 Apr. 2015 <http://www.amazon.com/Positivity-Top-Notch-Research-Reveals-Upward/dp/0307393747>

is the power or ability to return to the original form, position, etc., after being bent, compressed, or stretched; elasticity.[8]

In other words, when you become resilient you can bounce back from anything that you are dealing with. When you become resilient you learn that you have become anointed to bounce back no matter how hard you have been thrown down, you know that you are gonna bounce back from this situation. Your positive thoughts are connected to your resiliency. Look, you can allow your particular circumstance to deal you some very negative results. You can allow what you're dealing with to cause permanent damage to your mind. Permanent damage to your thought process. Permanent damage to how you act or how you respond to things.

Make a decision to hold fast and declare with your mouth, *"I am going to be positive, I am going to speak the word of God."* You can bounce back much quicker and better able to deal with detrimental situations and unwanted setbacks.

During Dr. Fredrickson's research, she discovered how positive emotions enable you to think more clearly. This is why David had to get that negativity out of his mind and pull from a positive mindset. He had to get his circumstance out of his mind. Because if he kept looking at the fact that everything was destroyed and that everything was burned down and

---

[8] "Resiliency | Define Resiliency at Dictionary.com." 2006. 22 Apr. 2015 <http://dictionary.reference.com/browse/resiliency>

that his family had been taken hostage, David might not have been able to recover like you will read at the end of the chapter. In spite of this situation being challenging to David, he learned quickly his first objective was to bounce back.

If we look over our lives we've been able to bounce back from some things that we may have previously been counted out with. We have been able to bounce back from things that we didn't think we would make it out of as well. And because of this epiphany, I can definitely define myself in one word, I am resilient.

As a matter of fact if I were sitting with you right now face to face, as I do with many women when I speak and minister, I often share with them as I will share with you, the importance of self-discovery. God has given each one of us a level of resilience to bounce back like a rubber ball or snap back into place like a rubber band. I don't know if you remember the game of jacks, but I considered myself one of the best. That little tiny ball that came with the jacks in a set was very versatile and could bounce in different directions, really high or really low depending on how hard you hit the ball on the ground. If you were a very skilled player like I was you could make that ball do all kinds of things in order to catch it just before it hit the ground you and your friends were playing on. That ball could go several feet into the air and come back down again and again if you were not quick to catch it.

In fact, I was that little girl that would purposely throw the ball down really hard to see how high it would go. The harder I threw it I found out quickly that the rubber ball would bounce back even higher than before. Now imagine yourself as the ball, being thrown down, hitting the ground, then suspended in the air and finally hitting the ground again if you had no one around to catch you; you could hit the ground multiple times before getting caught and secure in the hands of the Father. God has given us the same resilience as that jack's ball, having the ability to hit the ground, yet bouncing back over and over again.

It's a law, what goes up must come down. But guess what? You don't have to remain down. You can bounce back. God has you in His hands, and the reason many of us find ourselves hitting hard surfaces over and over is because we fail to stay in His hands. Which brings me back to that ball, remember, sometimes that little jacks ball would fall into our hands in our attempt to catch it, but on a few occasions we would not be fast enough and it would bounce off or our hand and roll on the ground. This same thing happens with us and God, we roll away, but thank God He comes and finds us in our landing place. Glory to God. Yes you must take on resilience, because the Bible says trials will come, persecutions will come, tribulations will come, and trouble will come, but God has given us a tough shell that is resilient for the ability to bounce back every time.

Deep inside I have a desire, and really want people to know that beyond the pictures, beyond the fame of what they think when they're looking at others, we often get impressions of what we think their life is like or what we think their life is about but I have been through so many different things that *I think people would say wow I can't believe she's that happy. I can't believe she smiles so much. I can't believe*...but it's because I imagine my nickname in the spirit is *resilient.*

As the Body of Christ, especially as a woman, we want to recover without permanent deformation. Although we can and will eventually recover from it... sometimes we think we have recovered from things but that permanent damage has been stuck with us so it causes us to have wrong mindsets. For example sometimes we experience damaged relationships it causes us to have permanent deformation of trust. Deformation of trust is best explained as when there is a force against us, or in many cases several forces against us, through us and all around us. Even though we have been rescued and resuscitated after the fact, we remain in the mindset of being a victim or victimized. Because of this deformation of our true character, we begin to have a problem with trusting people because of previous bad experiences (or coming out of one), but when you're resilient you learn how to come out of those same predicaments without allowing any of them to permanently damage you, especially your mind.

Many people admire the fact that I'm always smiling, but if I looked at my situation and the things that I've come through then I would have nothing to smile about. Over time I have discovered that I smile even more when I am processing what I have going on in the middle of the situation, more so than on the end. This is what David displayed to us as an example, when he stopped, assessed the situation he found himself in, and (although it was not his own fault) he stopped and encouraged himself. Let's think about it, how can we help anyone else around us, unless we can help ourselves? How on earth can God use you if you are a mess everyday and can't think straight about the simple daily task at hand. With this in mind, you have got to put on your resilience first before trying to process anything or you are going to make the mess you are in even bigger over time

Resilience in overload is the fuel that keeps an individual able to keep going in spite of critics or naysayers. Remember, your ability to bounce back depends solely on your level of faith and believing God that your breakthrough is within your grasp. Mental toughness is necessary during trying times. Keep reading below for more understanding, but in the meantime, you may have gotten knocked out, but your resilience or lack thereof will determine how long you decide to lay down, or how fast you decide to get up.

Before we move any further, please remember the following key points:

- Resiliency is the ability to bounce back without permanent damage.

- Positive emotions are important for resiliency and for being able to better deal with negative situations and setbacks.
- Positive emotions enables you to think more clearly and more creativity about how to handle and deal with the problems and situations.
- Negative emotions, as a rule, tend to constrict and limit your creativity and problem solving capabilities.

Over and over again within the word of God are reminders and responses to keep us anchored and resilient with the God gifted ability to always bounce back. We always win, triumph over our enemies and through the times of setbacks. God reminds us in His word to present our bodies as living sacrifices, holy and pleasing to Him, which is our reasonable service. If presenting our temples to him in a state of holiness is reasonable then I believe God would not command us to do anything that He would not give us the gift, talent or anointing to complete our assignments with. The psychological evaluation, which aligns significantly with this word that assures us we are already equipped with all that we need to stay positive.

Let everything that has breath, praise the Lord. Just as God gives us the ability to breathe, we also have the ability to praise. It is impossible to speak positive without breathing and the words we speak will always yield positive emotions and the outcome will also be positive as long as we think, behave and speak positive. But the point I would like to get across is this, when we remain in a positive state it allows us to think more clearly. It allows us to be able to think more freely according to her research and according to the word. Another example of this is when the Bible tells us to renew our mind and to renew our spirit on a consistent basis. That's because every day we're being clouded with negative images that are happening in the world.

As we view and review negative imagery played out by news media, we being clouded by situations and circumstances that our minds were not created to hold on to. The longer we remain clouded, the longer we're going to remain stuck in a situation; as long as we remain confused and lose the ability to focus due to the continuous barrage of a cloudy forecast. You will soon discover yourself tossing you to and fro as the Bible says, with every wind of doctrine, leaving you more confused operating in fear because you have no clarity of thought anymore.

The realization of having a made up mind is something you will have to do for yourselves and no one else can make up your mind for you. Finally when we put on a made up mind we are going to have positive emotions. This is what triggers our resiliency. Having your mind fixed and focus also triggers that bounce back spirit in you that lets you know that you know you are able to make it through this situation. You can finally take on the resolve in your spirit, soul and mind that you can come out of this condition and you won't have to stay there anymore.

When you put on resiliency you can boldly declare, *"I could be dealing with dark situations but I don't have to have a dark attitude. I could be dealing with negative stuff in my life but I don't have to have a negative attitude. I have to choose to have a positive mindset. I have to choose to have positive words coming out of my mouth. I have to choose to have a positive attitude towards what God is really ultimately trying to do through me."*

Sometimes in life, we get too stuck in what is happening to us versus trying to trigger our minds to line up to what God is ultimately trying to do through our lives. Because think about this, *how could you have a testimony without a test? How can we have victory if we never have storms?* God allows us to go through these storms and trials and tribulations and all of this to bring us to a greater place in Him. So, as we learn how to change our mindset declaring to ourselves, *"This trial is not going to kill me. This trial is not going to knock me out. This trial is not here to keep me here but I gotta learn how to press into that which God has for me."* This kind of mindset comes from thinking positive.

Let's pause right here, just think about the life of a superhero. A superhero has got to think to themselves, "I've got the power." I mean, without the ability (inward ability) to think positive with a winning attitude that they can win against whatever is coming her way. How can a superhero go before the villain already in defeat, before the battle even gets started? Over time, I just begin to just think positive... you know, when you have a positive attitude, it helps you to be able to see very clearly, remain calm at all times, and focus on the assignment you have been created for and when that setback moment arises in your life, you will already be prepared for your positive breakthrough on the other side.

Chapter VI

Process before the Promise

The Process is Only Temporary

Many times during your life, because God is sovereign He will often strategically place people in your life and in your midst that are going through some of the things that you have also gone through. And even in my life right now I am surrounded by many different women who are either going through a divorce or who are still broken after they've been divorced for umpteen years and haven't been able to move past their own pit moments. I am living proof that God can bring you up and out of a condition you may be facing right now and give you better than what you had before. I am living proof that you can make it out of a divorce or make it out of any type of dilemma even with experiencing the death of a family member in order to be able to know...when people look at me I am living proof of God bringing a person out of some of very dark moments.

I encourage you that whenever you look at me and see the smile on my face and witness that I'm going all out for God and giving Him praise and giving Him thanks, these are things that I do big in the midst of my situation and it is my desire that you take hold of some of my tenacity, some of my grit so to speak, even afar off, I can pull you out of your situation as well. You don't have to go through alone. Really you don't, let me explain in this way, *I am living proof that God is a keeper of His word.* The word of God reveals to us that the things we see currently are temporal and subject to change. But some of that change only happens when we make the determination that we are going to change our mindset about our situation.

A considerable number of us view our situations as *until death* but God didn't put anything in our lives until death. He allowed certain occurrences in our lives to help us to become stronger. Therefore, if we make an attempt to change our perception about what we are seeing and why we are going through the challenges we are facing and begin to learn how to trust God with what He's allowing us to experience; then at some point you can say to yourself *I was designed for this.*

Just realize, everything and I mean everything that God places you in was designed for that particular place and/or ideal circumstance. Uniquely as Christians we serve a God who is not a respecter of persons. He does not operate at a place where He loves me more than He loves you. So if He brought me out of all of my personal tribulations, He can certainly bring you out of your problems. No matter what you have been through and who you are, you can trust God.

First of all, there is always a process one has to endure before the promise. At this point in his life, David had already been anointed to be king and now he a fugitive on the run, Saul was in hot pursuit of him. Even within David's strength as a soldier fighting and winning in battle, there was still a process he had to go through. This is the same with you, in the middle of your process there are steps that you have got to take and things that you must go through in order to be able to see the promise fulfilled that God has for especially for you.

Particularly, God has promised you something but now it seems like those things are not going to work out. Now it seems that your situation is even worse as you begin to process who you really are. You're wishing that the prophet or the man or woman of God didn't even speak anything over your life. Because when they spoke that word over your life, you just knew that you were on your way. Then out of left field trouble showed up at your door to block you from receiving the promise. In the moment that word was released over your life, the prophecy went into motion and at the same time the enemy's divisive darts also went into motion. Please get this revelation, for every promise there is always going to be a problem and a process you will have to deal with and go through in order to receive it. I have found to be in this order... problem, process and then the promise.

God had it planned this way all along; as He stated to Jeremiah in Chapter 1 verse 5, let me remind you, *"I knew you before I formed you in your mother's womb. Before you were born I set you apart and appointed you as my prophet to the nations".* [9] David was holding on to a promise from God and refused to let go. He understood the promise came with persecution, the promise came with adversity and the promise came with sacrifice. When God calls you to a place of service in His Kingdom. Although we often embrace the calling on our lives as a privilege. We should also embrace the process as well. God called David at a young age and placed upon him a heavy responsibility. David learned early what the next generation would be assured of as always and will always be, the battle was already won and in the process you have to assume the posture of a winner at all costs. As you are going through your own process, remember this is not about you. This situation was a set up, God knew what you have coming over the horizon and has equipped you to receive the prophecy and the process so that ultimately you will capture the promise.

As David was walking out his process this was one of his darkest hours. When you are in the dark, there is a deep quiet, and in this deep quiet moment in your situation that seems to last a lifetime. In these dark

---

9 "Jeremiah 1:5 - "Before I formed you in the womb I - Bible ..." 2014. 29 Apr. 2015 <https://www.biblegateway.com/passage/?search=Jeremiah+1:5>

moments when it is difficult to get to sleep, our minds begin to visit our past mistakes and failures. In the dark when tend to have more time to reflect, and it is also in the dark moments of our lives that the enemy comes to remind us of our lowly place and also begin to download innuendos and impossibilities. We listen to him and begin to repeat and wash and repeat these untruths in our minds over and over again. Once we lose our minds over these disappointments, this is all we begin to think about. We find it difficult to come to grips with the truth anymore and unfortunately prefer the comfort of a lie in place of the truth, ultimately holding up the process because we begin to find comfort in our dark places. The bible does not really say how long David remained in process in the dark, but it does give a clear indication that it must have not been too long, because even in his process, he held on to the promise.

Yes it is possible to be in the dark and going through the process at the same time. Yes it is possible to be promised a thing from God right in the middle of your dark place.

But do you realize that your darkest moments come right before your promise?

Do you remember, midnight has to come before daybreak?

Do you know that things got to get worse before they get better?

Do you realize that when God says something, no matter what you gotta go through, it will surely come to pass?

David was holding on to his promise, and he began to encourage himself right there on the eve of his promise, and right there in the midnight of his process. Oftentimes we talk to God in our process this way, *Lord I know you said I'm gonna be healed but this pain just seem to be getting worse. Lord they're shifting me from doctor to doctor but God you said I'm gonna be healed. Father you said that I would have more than enough. I just lost my job but God I gotta keep holding on to this promise. Lord you said that this marriage was gonna work out but God they're acting like a straight fool. Lord you said that my children shall be blessed but it seems like they're getting in more trouble than ever.* But as you are speaking to God, remember it is also your own responsibility to hold on to your resilient resolve; nevertheless, no matter what, I am going to hold on to your promise. I am going to hold on to your promise.

Saints we have to shift our minds like David did in his hour of decision. Whenever you find yourself in a certain place of uncertainty, you have a decision to make.

Will I get crunk, or will I stay chill.

Will I light this place on fire with my mouth, or will I set the atmosphere and tone for peace in the midst of my storm.

David shifted his thoughts before his attitude shifted. You see, he had to make the determination, he had to access the situation he found himself in as it was no fault of his own. This was the situation he was dealt with, and acting a fool was not going to change the outcome, or so it seemed in that moment. When we find ourselves caught between two emotions going on deep inside of us, we must make the determination at that moment to honor God with our attitude, and honor ourselves and make the choice to chose the positive every time. This is the divine moment when your words can shape your entire future so just give yourself a pep talk and stick to your resolve to chose to *think*. David had to *think* this way.

Even though my situation appears negative, I am going to remain positive in spite of how things may look at this moment. .

Even though my situation may look upside down, I know that this is not the end of the road for me.

Even though things are breaking down and breaking loose, I know that what I'm seeing is only temporary.

To a great degree start telling your situation you are only temporary. Speak to your situation where you are and decree, "You are not gonna dictate how I feel this time. You are not gonna dictate what I think this time. You are not going dictate what I am this time. Because this time, if you do not speak it out of your mouth, you will continue to allow those negative occurrences and negative thoughts to continue to take over your dreams, your reality, your blessings and your life. And if you don't get a handle on your own outcome, take the spiritual reins, thus guiding your present circumstances with your tongue, then instantly, your own negative thoughts will become negative words and your negative words become negative actions. Ultimately, you will find yourself spiraling downward within a whirlwind of static negativity.

Always keep in mind, shift your thoughts, and shift your attitude. In doing so you may take hold of what God has already placed within your reach, God has already blessed you and given you what you are looking for, now your attitude will determine the outcome. God will give you what you're looking for, but following the process is major. Therefore, you must be willing to shift your thoughts and shift your attitude; this is critical for winning possession of the prize.

When I think about God allowing us to grasp the prize he has promised, first of all recognize the fact that we have need in the first place. How is it possible to receive anything with God without faith. Hebrews Chapter 11:6 states, *And without faith it is impossible to please Him.* [10] We have to realize that it's only through God that He allows us to be able to shift from one place through another place. *From darkness into light. From depression into a place absent of being afraid.* This should be our mantra, and it through Him and through His words that He allows us to be able to know as Our Father, He is not a God that won't give us what we're looking for or what we're asking for. He is a God who is aware of our most secret desires because

---

[10] "Hebrews 11:6 - And without faith it is impossible to - Bible ..." 2011. 29 Apr. 2015 <https://www.biblegateway.com/passage/?search=Hebrews%2011:6>

He is the one that put all desires within each one of us. *Everything that we're looking for. Everything that we're dreaming of. Everything that we're going after that's in our hearts*, was specifically placed within our hearts. And as He's placed those things in our hearts there's a process from when we get from one point to another one.

Mentally, we must learn how to do this, making that mind shift and moving into a place of choice. We all have a choice, it may not come easily to some as others, but first of all when I think of shifting my mind and shifting my attitude this movement that comes from within, confirms my position and solidifies that choice...I have to make the choice. In order to shift personally, you have to make a choice. You have to make a decision and sometimes your circumstances won't always line up with that decision to shift. What I mean by shifting in your mind, the Bible brings clarity in us to be not conformed to the by the renewing of our mind. In order to get from one place to another place we have to learn how to change our mind and our attitude towards the situation. Many times the reason why we're stuck in certain things is because we have allowed our minds, on a subconscious level, to dictate to us where we are. For instance, if you are desiring a new job but you had the door closed in your face after going on several interviews, once this happens, a required shift inside my mind exists, and it doesn't matter how many interviews I've go on, one of these interviews is going to land me the job that I'm believing God for. When we secure a decision solidly in our mind, that enables us to stand flat footed saying, *"I absolutely will not be in this place and this position any more.*

After standing on the Word, speaking in faith, and believing what we said is so in the moment those words left our lips, we begin to understand how a lot of changes in our personal life start with a simple mind change. Our perception of a thing, conceives our reality. Once the thought is conceived, then that same thought, whether negative or positive responds and gives birth to our misfortune or fortune instantaneously. Our thoughts normally create responses and actions, and if we begin to think a particular way, we decide the destiny of our own response to the situations and circumstances of our true conditions.

A particularly interesting personal instance I recall happening in my life , a lot of times my responses to different experiences would cause people to tell me, *I was mean or mean spirited*. Finally, I began to look at myself closely and examine how I would often respond either directly or indirectly at events unfolding around me. Almost reluctantly at first, but over time I knew a mind shift was in order, and the only way I knew to change my thinking was to get into the word of God. Anger has a way of masking itself on the inside of you, and anger acts as a chameleon, hiding and adapting to whatever it needs to, but if left hidden will return to it's origin. Let me explain, in some instances we know it is impossible to act up, scream, yell, argue. Most people who are angry will not remove the mask they are wearing in church, or even in a place of business but once they got home they would remove that mask. While the chameleon is in hiding, it will not reveal it's true or natural colors, but once it returns to the safety of it's natural habitat it will return to it's normal appearance. This is representative of how anger also hides behind bitterness, resentment, jealousy, envy, and strife but if left unchecked for a period of time, or caught off guard, will present in a mean spirited attitude. Get the picture?

After enough people tell you about your condition, even in a state of denial, you can hear the truth, although you may not be as willing to accept it at the time. But over a period of time, experiences periods of hurt and pain, there comes a time to self-reflect.

Of course I was operating in the spirit of anger. But I found out that the precursor to anger was fear, and God does not give us the spirit of fear. 2 Timothy Chapter 1:7 confirms this, *"For God has not given us the spirit of fear (timidity), but of power and love and a sound mind."* [11] Before this scripture verse 7 reminds us to *stir up* our *spiritual* gifts and this is something only we can do for ourselves. I had to make this shift on my own, in order to shift me from operating in a spirit of anger to having joy or having peace or

---

[11] "2 Timothy 1:7 KJV - For God hath not given us the spirit of ..." 2014. 29 Apr. 2015 <https://www.biblegateway.com/passage/?search=2+Timothy+1%3A7&version=KJV>

having happiness which would eventually change my attitude and mood.

Personally, I had to get into the word on anger and I had to look up the word of God on scripture that pertained to anger. Once I found out that the word of God instructs us to avoid being angry about anything. Once the Word showed me how anger should not be my regular demeanor I started putting pressure on my mindset, eventually, my mind started the big shift regarding me and change began saturate my mind and my thoughts began to change my words and my words began to change my actions. Once my actions changed, my outer appearance began to change. People noticed my countenance changed. Some of you don't realize how anger is seen in your countenance. Our countenance is the conception of how God views us inwardly, but is reflected in our outer appearance. Countenance is defined as the appearance of a person's face: a person's expression.[12]

Once Cain slew Abel as noted in Genesis Chapter 4:6 allow me to paraphrase the conversation between God and Cain within my spiritual imagination. God called Cain after He heard Abel's blood cried out to Him, once He found Cain in hiding He asked this question, "Cain, why are you hiding? Where is your brother? What have you done to Him? Why is that expression on your face? Stop giving me that side-eye

---

[12] "Countenance | Definition of countenance by Merriam-Webster." 2005. 29 Apr. 2015 <http://www.merriam-webster.com/dictionary/countenance>

stare! What is your problem? Why are you indignant? I conclude this matter firmly, God saw all over Cain's face his anger that was so deeply rooted causing him to murder his own blood. Was he sorrowful, of course not, was he depressed, possibly...but at the end of the day he was guilty as charged and anger was his downfall. We must step out of the sinful garments of anger and fear and step into the garments of praise, which can only happen for us if we shift our minds from fear to faith.

Chapter VII

Dead Garments

Generally speaking, dead garments are some of the clothing we wore when we were in the world, before salvation and before our new birth. Garments can be described as those type of issues we have and what we have been through. When we talk about garments, a lot of times our facial expressions, a lot of times what we do, what we say is a derivative...a direct derivative of what we're wearing on the inside. Examples of dead garments: fear, anger, depression, bitterness, etc. Intellectually speaking, we know death can only apply physically to a person biologically and once all functions in the physical body has terminated. But I am speaking of garments or clothing that we wear in the spirit. This is applied to spiritually dead, pre-salvation state, or a state of consciousness when we did not know Jesus. The absence of relationship with the Father and having the knowledge of Jesus Christ as our Lord and Savior, comes from a state of being dead spiritually. These dead clothes were a sure indication of my position with God, being totally outside of His will and His ways.

The funny thing about these so called dead garments is that many of us still wear them even after our conversion over to Christ. Most of that is because we haven't spiritually matured in many of the areas of our lives that require us to develop. Even though we were saved from the curse of hell by salvation, there is still a process of growth that we must manage throughout our daily Christian walk. Dead garments are simply wrong attitudes and mindsets that we have walked in for years that are going to require effort on our part along with the word of God, and much assistance from the Holy Spirit in order for true maturity to take place. Let me take the pressure off of you in your mind, it doesn't happen overnight. It takes time to see true transformation or in other words spiritual maturity to take place. However as Christians we should desire to change in order to represent our heavenly Father in the earth.

I too wore these dead clothes, but thankfully, I did not have to continue in that state. God always give us a substitute when we find Him, we then know Him and we can take off those dead garments and put on the garment of praise! Hallelujah!

Specifically, I believe that praise is an outward expression of an internal resolution. Therefore every time we come into the presence of others or a place of worship; whatever garment we have on people can really see them. *Am I feeling depressed? That's what people are seeing. So that's the clothing that I'm walking in.* But, if I make a decision to shift my mind and shift my heart and put a smile on my face before anyone has to pump me up, including encouraging myself to give God praise in spite of what I'm dealing with and in spite of what I'm going through. *Now I am wearing new garments. Now my garments are a smile, a right attitude, praise on my lips, hands lifted, and of course my kodak smile.* However you decide you're going to feel on the inside, that's what we'll be able to see on the outside.

Some of us are quite capable of getting positively shifted in any situation, yet there are others who still find this challenging and difficult. How do we actually get there, into the shift?

Getting into the shift often comes along with an expectation. Expecting a move from God alone is a powerful affirmation, but expecting a demand from ourselves is a pivotal turning point.

Well for me, when I'm expecting from God, first of all, as believers, we have to know how to pray and command the blessings God has already promised to come to pass in our lives. *And without expectation, there is no vision.* We have to fix our mind on that thing in order to see it manifest in our lives. Then without clarity of vision, how can I think…how can I receive properly what God says He wants to do in my life? So I have to create an atmosphere in my own personal life in order to be able to expect God to do anything concerning my personal expectation.

For example, if I enter into a particular place like my place of employment and complete my duties required of me, at the end of the work week I expect to get a check in my hand or via direct deposit into my checking account of choice. Many of us go to work, sowing 40 hours or more per week, and expect to be paid on time, without exception. Most of us don't consider the matter at all, never staying up all night wondering, *will I get paid this payday? We don't lose an ounce of brain cells thinking about the possibility of not getting paid. The reason we think like that is because we expect to get paid and if we don't there is going to be trouble.* In this exact same way, we should have the same expectation when we are standing on *the word of God to come to pass in our lives. See trading your dead garments is not as hard as you might have thought but it will require expectation and a shift in your mind in order to see results.*

If the Word of God says that I am above only and never beneath. [13]

If the word of God says that He made me the head and never the tail[14].

Then I am expecting God to do something major in my life!

Most people, unfortunately never expect God to do anything for them. Just going through the motions, you

---

[13] "Deuteronomy 28:13 The LORD will make you the head, not..." 2013. 29 Apr. 2015 <http://biblehub.com/deuteronomy/28-13.htm>

[14] "Deuteronomy 28:13 - The LORD will make you the head, not ..." 2014. 29 Apr. 2015 <https://www.biblegateway.com/passage/?search=Deuteronomy+28:13>

know, on a day to day basis. Others are merely living the same old hum drum lives and void of the presence of God, making the same tired excuses and never ever placing a demand on their own expectations of Him to do anything in their lives. Ephesians Chapter 3:20 clarifies God's abilities in our lives, *Now unto him who is able to do exceedingly abundantly above all that we ask or think, according to the power that worketh in us.*[15] Therefore, God has placed everything in Him inside of us, so we should always be in a place of expectancy.

Part of expecting from God comes with becoming more observant of my surroundings, I had to learn to look at me because often when I entered into a room, ironically I automatically felt that people just didn't like me. Yes that was me feeling as if the moment I entered any room, anywhere, people just turned up their nose or frowned up as if I had body odor. Of course I did not smell because I wear the finest perfumes, and I bathe this temple, but there must have been this invisible aura around me that offended most of the people I came in contact with. One day God spoke plainly to me and said *"Nobody's even thinking about you. That's in your mind. That's in your mind."*

The mind can cause you to see and hear things that are not actually there. The Bible refers to these thoughts in 2 Corinthians 10:5 as *vain imaginations*

---

[15] "Ephesians 3:20 Now to him who is able to do immeasurably ..." 2013. 29 Apr. 2015 <http://biblehub.com/ephesians/3-20.htm>

or high things[16] *that raise themselves above things about God and ourselves that we really don't know or understand.* We can have a *battlefield* right inside of us, inside of our own minds. I giggle as I think about the arguments that have literally gone on inside of me. Some people refer to this a talking to yourself. Folks would call you crazy if they were to audibly hear the conversations going on in our minds.

Why is she looking at me? Do I stink? I know I look good, she's just jealous. If they look over here one more time, I'm going to light this joint up! They don't like me. I don't fit in here. No one understands me.

I can go on and on with the absurdities we often allow to swim around in our thoughts. The struggle is real, but it does not have to affect us, if we only learn to take authority over our own mind.

Here's another example of what I am speaking of.

If I am simply walking in a room that everyone else was sitting in before I arrived; what causes me to think negatively about the people that are in the room? Because guess what? That stinking thinking started with me. It started with me.

Now in my mind, I'm thinking, not all but some of the people in the room don't like me at all. *Can I possibly remain positive even if they don't like me? Do I have to allow your bad attitude to shift on my attitude? The answer is no! Do I have to allow how you think and*

---

16 "2 Corinthians 10:5 KJV - Casting down imaginations, and ..." 2014. 29 Apr. 2015 <https://www.biblegateway.com/passage/?search=2+Corinthians+10%3A5&version=KJV>

how you feel to dictate what I'm going to do and how I'm going to access the kingdom of God? No, not at all.

I am focusing so much on the mind as it pertains to dead garments because if our minds aren't freed we will continue even as Christians to walk in emotions such as distress, fear, discouragement, anger just to name a few. A part of embracing a change of heart and receiving good things from God is learning how to control your mind and continue to expect God's word to make a difference in your execution of it in your lives. Practice does make perfect, so take some time out to train your brain spiritually with the same tenacity you have already done physically. Teaching your mind how to respond as well as how to react is part of becoming a mature adult. No more playing small.

Some of you simply need a time out!

It is time out for playing in the sandbox and not sharing your toys.

It is time out for blaming other people for what is happening in your own life.

It is time out for looking at your circumstances and allowing those negative emotions to rule your response or reactions

Remember, David's men played the blame game (they wore dead garments). But guess what David decided to do? David decided to take off those garments and began to take charge of his own thinking. They turned outward and started blaming David for what they were going through but David decided in his own mind, *I'm not gonna blame anybody, not even myself, and I refuse to blame God. I'm just going to go down in my repertoire of victories. I'm just gonna dig deep on the inside because I know I got some testimony of my own where I could have my own church service from how good God has been . Just thinking about God brought me from being a shepherd to getting ready to be a king. God I just wanna thank you for allowing me to know that I will come out of this situation and have all that you have promised.*

Did y'all know that David wasn't even in the lineup? When Samuel came to anoint him as king they didn't even think enough of David to bring him to the lineup. Every time David went through something it always seemed like he was rejected or he was always left out or he was always overlooked. But guess what? David refused to walk in those dead garments of rejection but he put on a spirit of praise and began to encourage himself.

Expectancy is one important change in your mindset that you need because everything you have had to deal with up to this point was meant to happen for a particular moment in God's timing. Once you arrive to that particular moment you must be ready and able to pull out all of your memories from your past into this moment, just to help you get over that hump of doubt and unbelief that tries to rear their ugly head and distract you from your course towards the finish line. No one else can pull from your past for you, you must be ready to recall and sometimes recite your own testimony.

This week some of you will go through an experience that will make you cry out, "*Really God?*" Yes I hear you loud and clear, you don't think I am writing to you, I must be talking about someone else. Trust me, I am not speaking negative into your life, this is my attempt to keep you from being caught off guard when you experience your own personal Ziklag moment. Anyone who has walked with God long enough, I can say with all honesty, most if not all, have already experienced a dark moment when they too have asked the question, "*Really God?*" These are the moments when your faith is tested the most, and you are going to learn how to encourage yourself.

Some of you all are in some deep stuff right now. Use this book as guide to give you some wisdom, and also remember to read your Bible.

First of all recall your past situation, learn how to look at what you've been through already and keep it moving.

Secondly, you must implement understanding and practice how to line your heart up, your mouth up, your mind up and your lifestyle up with the word of God.

David did all of the above. These practices were all ways of him shifting out of those dead garments into garments of praise!!!

Jesus did not die on the cross so you could live a distressed and depressed life, nor to live in grave clothes for eternity. He didn't give His life so that you could be stressed and anxious, nor full of negative emotions always following you throughout the course of your life. Jesus died so that you could have life and live an abundant life[17]!

God promises you and me an abundant life, as written in John Chapter 10:10

reads, "I have come so that they may have life and have it in abundance."[18]

In addition to just living life hum drum, God says He wants us to have more than abundance alone, but "more abundance." You can just tell your situation, *you are only temporary. I am only in this for this moment. I am only in this because of what God has purposed and planned for my life.*

I just want to encourage your hearts today in order to release some good word into your hearts, sow a seed of life into your mind, and give you a little help in your press to enable you to shift. But there is one thing I cannot do for you, and that is give self-encouragement. You have got to learn how to encourage yourself, by yourself. You have to do this when folks are in with you and when they are out (on AWOL) in your life. Give pity party an eviction notice today and firmly say no to what the devil is trying to get you to give up on. Instead of rehearsing the curse the devil tried to plant in your generation, tell this yourself, *this sickness is not until death.* This is only a temporary health challenge that I'm going through

---

[17]"John 10:10 The thief comes only to steal and kill and destroy ..." 2013. 30 Apr. 2015 <http://biblehub.com/john/10-10.htm>

[18]"John 10:10 The thief comes only to steal and kill and destroy ..." 2013. 30 Apr. 2015 <http://biblehub.com/john/10-10.htm>

and this *sickness is not until death.* Speak out loud and with boldness declaring, *This cancer is not gonna beat me.* Whatever it is that I'm dealing with. *This is not going to beat me because I've been through some other things and God if you brought me out of them you will bring me out of this.*

In this moment I simply want to encourage you to change your garments. Turn pity into praise and expect to see the hand of God move in your life. Let's go through the process together.

Chapter VIII

A Woman After God's Own Heart

"*Really God?*" symbolizes an emotionally surprising and shocking feeling directed only towards God that expresses the thought, *"I can't believe this is happening to me."* In some phase of my life I felt like I've been doing everything I was supposed to do. *I was praying. I was reading. I was studying. I was preaching. I was ministering. I was tithing. I was giving.* I felt I was doing everything I was supposed to do, and all of the sudden my life turned upside down. In my attempt to paint a picture here for you, I was knocked off of my proverbial platform and then was down for the count. I could actually see the enemy with his boxing gloves standing over me with a smirk on his face. But even though I was my low place, I remembered the sovereignty of God and I knew everything happens in His perfect timing.

My ex and I began our relationship during my senior year in high school. He was older than I, and we dated for quite a while (on and off) before we got married. After about eight years of marriage, we both came to the realization our marriage was not working out. The odd part about our breakup, we were not connecting as a couple should, and no matter how much counseling we sought after, our marriage needed resuscitating, no actually a miracle was in order to save us. Sorry I don't have any dirt for you, there was no cheating involved from either side, it just did not work. Our covenant binding was severed, the disconnect seemed to be as I reflect, we were two individuals heading in two different directions and our paths didn't cross anymore. I wanted to pursue my calling in ministry and he at that time seemed disinterested in everything. We simply grew apart and I know you are thinking, that sounds so cliche' but seriously this is the truth. I'm my opinion I grew up and he wanted to remain the same.

For the most part, earlier on in our marriage we seemed to flow well, but you know I can't place my finger on a certain thing that caused us to lose touch with what we had during the early times. So one day out of the blue my husband came home and reported he had lost his job. That put our family in a deep financial bind, of course leaving me to figure out how we were going to go from two salaries to one and juggle all of the other responsibilities. Honestly reflecting back it seemed as if I had most of the responsibilities by myself. When I got the news he had lost his job and he was so nonchalant about it ..I was done. I realized that a person can be in the house with you and still not be with you. Present in body but mind and heart so far away. That's what we were to each other.

Previously, we were very close, but from my viewpoint, it seemed the closer I got to God as I stepped out further in the deep in ministry, the more apart we became when my expectations of our intended direction did not seem to go as I planned. I really thought we were on one page with our goals in ministry and our focus was to move forward as one, but over time I begin to notice the signs that he wanted nothing to do with ministry and at that point I wanted nothing to do with this marriage. If this had not been disheartening to me, you know, how you are really expecting your spouse to be there for you, well at least excited about what God is doing in your life, instead I did not expect the reaction from someone who I had been with most of my life. I realized that we were becoming more toxic to each other and it was affecting our children negatively so I decided to file for divorce.

Here I was in the middle of a divorce, operating in a leadership roll in my church and then asked to leave. Let me pause right here, because, I was actually kicked out and there is no nicer way to explain the situation I found myself in. Two parallel events that disturbed my spirit and wrecked my mind, sending me in a downward spiral of unbelief. I am speaking of a church I helped the leaders build, a church where I was one of the key leaders. Then one day, all of the sudden, I became arch enemy number one *because the people were calling my name too much*. I was also told, *we need you to leave because people don't know who the real leaders are here.*

The point I am driving here, all of this occurred in the same season and on top of all of that drama, my father dies. The morning of his death we spoke to one another, and in the same afternoon my Dad has a heart attack and collapsed and died on his desk. The events all spiraled like a tornado and it all happened so fast, so it I was taken off guard. You understand? We get so caught up in the trivial matters in life, and forget to pay closer attention to the important stuff. Call it karma, call it fate, call it payback if you want but remember with every action there is a reaction. The storm came through too quickly and I could not catch my breath between one tragic outcome after another. Come on look at the irony, to be at one church for 5 years and be asked to leave. That particular Sunday I was prepared to teach Sunday School, but instead of experiencing a worship experience, I arrive to an empty building to be politely asked to leave. Everyone got the email, text message but me I supposed, because no one showed up but me and my soon to be ex-husband that morning.

After the complete and utter dismay the thoughts that were swimming in my mind as I tried to grasp what was happening in that moment. *These are people you served. You loved. You carried their bags. You're tithing to their ministry. You gave them your heart. They were the godparents of your children and then just out of the blue you're asked to go.*

Being told to lie to the membership about my departure took me to a whole new level. *Oh by the way, I am starting my own ministry, my season is up, I'm offended, I've outgrown this teaching, I'm relocating across town(All lies I was asked to tell the lay members).* I was so confused and really did not know what to say when people asked, because whatever I had to say would be a flat out lie, and I couldn't understand why, this had to happen now. Really God?!! Really?!!

My marriage dissolved, kicked out of church, and now just like that my father is gone. *My father was my mentor. He was my friend. He was my heart.* Now who can help me sort the pieces out in this puzzle. My father was only 49 years old when he died from his second heart attack. And as I stated, that morning when we talked on the phone my last words to my dad were *I love you* and that was a prompt to the pressing of the Holy Spirit to tell him that because he was getting ready to hang up the phone and I stopped him beforehand saying, *Dad, I love you.* Not having a clue these words would be my last to my father. I discussed everything with him, he coached me in ministry and was the greatest father.

The late Bishop A. C Speakman (my father-in-law), once said to me, "*Orienthia you have a knack for making your misery your ministry*, a*nd because you're willing and comfortable being transparent with the people, God is gonna give you a platform to do ministry with that.*" Thus, *CR8NME Ministry* was later birthed because I had no issues with helping people even if it meant sharing very personal parts of my testimony Psalm Chapter 51:10 [19]states, Create in me a clean heart oh God, and renew a right spirit within me. This is the basis of my women's ministry. Our vision is to inspire , motivate, and empower women to transition from a place of brokenness , stagnation, and complacency to the God ordained purpose in life.

David is a man that wasn't perfect but he served a perfect God. A man that realized he had blood on his hands but he was still able to be used for Kingdom building. A man who loved God with all his heart and if people looked at his resume they would say that he is totally disqualified for that attribute But God saw something even more valuable in David than his actions. God looked at his heart. And even though his actions weren't always right, his heart relayed to God that he was indeed *a man after God's own heart.*

A while back, I remember asking God this question. *How can you choose somebody like David and say if he's a man after your heart* [20]*this man that killed more people than any other man in the Bible?* How could you choose him as the apple of your eye[21]? This man had adultery and did all these things, why was he chosen? In addition, the word also tells us that *God doesn't*

19"Psalm 51:10 - Bible Gateway." 2014. 1 May. 2015 <https://www.biblegateway.com/passage/?search=Psalm+91%3A10-12&version=KJV>

20"Man After Your Own Heart (Gary Chapman Cover) - YouTube." 2012. 14 May. 2015 <http://www.youtube.com/watch?v=u0jzhyoS76s>

21"Psalm 17:8 Keep me as the apple of your eye; hide me in ..." 2013. 14 May. 2015 <http://biblehub.com/psalms/17-8.htm>

look at the outward appearance of man, he looks at our heart.[22] And God wants every person to realize that most of the situations that we face are temporary. We may be going through our distressed hour, our pit moment, our process and especially our thank you party's. This journey is a matter of the heart, it's a heart thing so to speak. What's your heart looking like on that area or that arena because at the end of the day that's where God is looking at our heart.

Speaking of our heart, the heart actually reveals the timing of God. When our hearts can be found pure and ready to receive God totally into our circumstances this is usually the time He steps in and takes the reign in our relationships, our circumstances and our condition. God's timing is absolutely perfect and complete, missing nothing.

---

22 "1 Samuel 16:7 But the LORD said to Samuel, "Do not ..." 2013. 1 May. 2015 <http://biblehub.com/1_samuel/16-7.htm>

Chapter IX

It's Time to Get My Life

Now is the time to get your life. You deeply thought you lost time, but in fact you may had added more time to your life. (Yes allow that to marinate a bit.) Did I forget to mention in the previous chapter that God was, is and always will be a time redeemer? Don't sit around pouting about the time you wasted, or the time you lost! God had extended His grace on you and you still have time to get your life.

Strange thing about time is we often believe we don't have enough, have plenty or we just don't believe God is answering fast enough. We ask, "When God, when?" I love Ecclesiastes answer to our undying question about when will the answer to our problems finally arrive.

"To everything there is a season, a time for every purpose under heaven." Ecclesiastes 3:1 [23]

---

[23] "Ecclesiastes 3:1 - Bible Gateway." 2014. 4 May. 2015 <https://www.biblegateway.com/passage/?search=Ecclesiastes+3%3A1&version=NKJV>

Allow me to repeat, there is a time for everything that occurs under heaven and God's timing for our lives, God has a time for every purpose, and so now with that being said, *it is time to get your life*!

Before we can go and get our life *back,* well first of all, one of the things that we have to realize is that we have to get grounded within our mind, we are going to be in pursuit of all that God says that we can have. We have to make up our minds and know without a doubt we will be in pursuit of what God says we can surely have. In all of my study of the Bible, I cannot find anywhere; God never told us that we are supposed to stay stuck in a rut. God never told us that we're supposed to stay stuck in and accepting bad situations in our lives. God never told us that it was ok to sit around becoming stagnant. But God did let us know that we are supposed to be in pursuit of those things that He tells us that we need to be in pursuit of. For example, if God tells you to start a business, write a book, join a ministry, start a church then this is what you need to be planning and doing until He comes.

For reasons like these we have to make up in our mind that we desire everything God says we can have. How do you know what God says you can have? You find the promises of God in His word and you keep repeating the Word He spoke to you over and over until you see them manifest. Another thing you must do to is find the situation and circumstance in His word that you can identify with. The Bible contains 66 books of words of encouragement. Inside the pages, it gives us life, and whatever we need to move forward and take action. The Word of God is our lifeline.

Far too many times to count in my own life, I have had to arm myself with the tools found inside each scripture specific to my experience. I purchased a concordance and begin to look up the words that I did not understand fully and studied until I could grasp hold of the meaning and gain full understanding in the areas where God was speaking to my heart. Some of you reading this may feel God is far off somewhere and can never relate with what you are going through, but I am a witness, He can be found right on the pages of the Bible. You see the scriptures come alive when you read them, when you did for answers like treasure deep under the ground. If you just keep on digging you will find your answers. Not only will you find your answers but you will keep on digging, but let me warn you, you will never get enough!

The word of God must be foremost in all of our lives, so as I am ministering to someone, I always take them to what God says about the matter. My opinion may help you for a while, but God's word will help you for a lifetime. Yes, I have to take you to the raw, uncut, unadulterated, uncompromised word of God. The written word of God. Prophecies will come and they are good. Preached Sermons are also good. Listening to positive faith confessions are also real good. But getting in the word of God and studying His word for yourself is even better.

Let me repeat, opening up your bible, getting your concordance out and going in on whatever area in your life you are having an issue with.

Do you need to get your life back in your finances? Then find scripture after scripture and begin to confess those scriptures over your life and gain more understanding over what God's financial principles are in this particular area

Do you need to *get your life back in getting over or moving past that state of dealing with the loss of a family member?* God gives us encouragement such as gaining peace and joy in the midst of those type of losses.

Do you need to get your life back in the area of your health? God promises healing in His word, just take those scriptures that deal with healing and consume them within your mind and heart until you see your healing manifested.

For every issue we may experience in our lives, God has a principle in His word to answer or solve it. The Word of God has every key you will ever need for unlocking your future and moving past anything. Because if we're gonna renew our minds, we cannot renew our minds with all that old information blocking our destiny. We must first and foremost get in pursuit of the promises found in the Word. Find out whatever the promise says we should have and begin to work our way through that and then once we get into the word we can now create positive confessions that we can say to ourselves on a daily basis until we see victory in a particular area in our life.

As believers we also have Holy Spirit to lead, guide and teach us His word by expounding and guiding us into all truth. John 16:13 states, *"Howbeit when he, the Spirit of truth, is come he will guide you into all truth... He will tell you only what he has heard from me, and he will not speak on his own authority, but whatever he hears, that he will speak, and show you what is to come."*[24]

So you see we have help so there is no reason to struggle in gaining understanding of God's word, when has sent you help! Now, get your life in the area of seeking God's word, seeking answers to strengthen you in your situation and move you into your amazing future. The more your study the word of God and apply it to your life, soon you will see your way out and on to a successful life.

We get our life when we are chosen by God. David was chosen out of all of his brothers, by God, even if He was not considered by men. In this case, his own father Jesse did not think David was ready for obvious reasons. He was young, inexperienced, he hung out with the sheep as a mere herder, and he was not even in position when his name was mentioned. [25]Listen, there is a meeting going on and your name is being

---

[24]"John 16:13 - Bible Gateway." 2012. 4 May. 2015 <https://www.biblegateway.com/verse/en/John%2016:13>

[25]"1 Samuel 16 - Samuel Anoints David - The LORD said to..." 2014. 4 May. 2015 <https://www.biblegateway.com/passage/?search=1+Samuel+16>

mentioned. You are not even in the vicinity, but God is whispering your name in the ear of someone who has the pull, who makes hiring decisions, who is the President or CEO of a corporation that needs your anointing or the process cannot go forward. You never know what can happen when you decide to get your life and move when you hear your name, but remember you must be ready. Never allow your past experiences to count you out, you are qualified and you are chosen.

I can even imagine how David must have felt once he did come because they didn't give David time to wash up. They didn't give David time to get his mind together or anything. They sought after David from the field and brought him to the lineup. I can imagine the rejection that David might have felt all of those years with not just that but he was the only one out there you know, shepherding the sheep, all alone with possibly minimal assistance.

As I reflect on my own life right now, there has been many times where I have been overlooked for positions and given the excuse, *"Well, you're not pretty enough. You're not good enough. You weigh too much. You're too short. This is just not for you. You're loud. You don't articulate your words properly. Your hair is not long enough. You don't have the...your family don't have enough money.* There are so many flat out lies that the enemy uses to try to keep you out of the ultimate position that God has for you. And so He uses weapons such as, rejection, bitterness, and depression. He uses every weapon in his arsenal that will attempt to keep us out of our rightful position where God ultimately has for us to be in our own personal lives.

No matter what the enemy tried to do to him, David was destined to be king because God appointed him as king. Once the King's edict goes forth, it's over, it's a wrap you are who God says you are...period. Now it's time to go and get your life! God has spoken, His word has gone forth and no matter what you did in the past nor what you will do in the future will stop whatever word or promise God has put into motion. It is what it is and the only person that can stop it is you by not moving when the word is spoken. Going through trials can't stop you, you are destined, so go and get your life!

Before I close this chapter I must mention these verses: I Sam. 30:7-8

"Then David said to Abiathar the priest, the son of Ahimelech, "Please bring me the ephod." So Abiathar brought the ephod to David. 8 David inquired of the LORD, saying, "Shall I pursue this band? Shall I overtake them?" And He said to him, "Pursue, for you will surely overtake them, and you will surely rescue all." 9So David went, he and the hundred men who were six with him,

These scriptures make me feel like I wanna run, as the church folk would say. After David encouraged himself, got his mind right, and grabbed hold of his resilience, he is now ready to seek the Lord for His next steps. Some of you need to read that sentence again because at some point in our walk we have to stop going to God crying and whining. We need to go to our heavenly father with our mind in the right place so we can properly hear from him.

David was a soldier by trade so fighting another battle was not a problem. David recognized that this situation needed the voice of God. David could have went straight into war but he wanted to make sure God was on his side. Once David got God's approval to pursue and recover all, David went right into action. This should be how we operate as it pertains to adversity in our lives. Getting your life is a phrase that I coined that means to get in pursuit of what God told you to do! Pursuit is when you make up in your mind that you will do whatever it takes to make sure that assignment is completed.. overtaken. When God speaks, we need to be obedient. In that obedience you are surely unstoppable in obtaining every promise God has given to you. Let me reiterate 3 important points found in these particular scriptures for you because I believe they are vital in assisting you to go from setback to bounce back!!

- David didn't rely on his own knowledge or wisdom, he sought God.
- Once David inquired of God, he waited for specific instructions on what to do in this particular situation
- David moved quickly on God's instruction

Chapter X

Behind the Kodak Smile

Behind my smile is my authentic self and it is not fake, it is truly real. Honestly speaking, I am not putting on a face or a smile nor am I merely just striking a pose. Because you live through a storm and survived several others does not mean that every day is going to be a happy day. But it does mean that when you recognize and really, really truly recognize that you are going to come out of this storm system, no matter what and whether it ends up the way that I want it to or if it goes in another direction then I had planned for, I have to go along in order to get to the promise that God has prepared especially for me.

Why...you ask? Because God promised. So if I keep that kodak smile, maintain my positive attitude and remain in faith and focused on Jesus, I now take the pressure off me and place it all on God.

Some promises from God are simply in the *waiting stages*. God is just processing us for our next level. It's kind of like desiring to purchase a new car but I don't have the money right at this moment, so I come up with a plan to work on a second or third job and do all of this extra work because I'm feeling the pressure of making my desire for a new car come to pass on my time, knowing all along, that God says to wait on His timing.

As we are going through many different bounce back processes or opportunities, *we want that process to happen fast. You know we want this to be over tomorrow. We don't wanna deal with this hurt too much longer. We don't wanna deal with this pain.*

Oftentimes the process is just too much, especially when we know too well, and there is not anything we can do about it apart from God. *You know it's not about our faith. It's not about obedience. It's about the timing of God.* And I understand, when we are going through hard times, we don't wanna have this kind of conversation with ourselves because we think that if we speak it...you know we have voices in our head that tells us, *you don't have enough faith because this hasn't manifested or that particular prophecy hasn't come to pass. You don't have enough things because certain events haven't happened.* Or maybe church folks whisper in our ears, *You're not obedient enough because this hasn't happened.* Well let me encourage you today, all of the above could be...wrong...dead wrong. Most of the time, it is just, the timing of God.

Let me speak to you directly. I cannot sugar coat this information I am about to share with you and it is so simple a child would understand it.. YOUR breakthrough is in your praise!! Your breakthrough is one praise away from God giving you what it is that you're looking for but you have been hanging out in the "Complaint Department" instead of on the "Praise Team." Yes sometimes its just that simple and we are sometimes just too stubborn to be obedient to the simplicity of God's word so we miss out! But in addition your breakthrough is also in your attitude and in your thought processes. Basically, how you think will dictate how long you remain in the process. Have you ever heard the saying, your attitude determines your altitude, well I am a firm believer in that. Earlier I wrote about my smile, if you ran into me unplanned in the grocery story, I'm always happy. I refuse to only smile at church, and I refuse to post fake selfies on Facebook. I choose to live a happy life. Being in a state of happiness is a choice you will have to make right now. *Not because everything will always be right. Not because everything is the way that you want it to be at this moment.* But because I know who I serve and I know *if He brought me out before He'll bring me out this time. If He brought me to it He'll bring me through it.* And some of us wear the baggage that we're going through on our backs, and another point I want to make right here, we need to stop wearing the wrong garments. Check yourselves, make sure you are wearing the right garments. I'm just giving you an opportunity to give God praise and take the blinders off. Take the time to remove the wrong garments, and just thank God for what he's getting ready to do.

I am excited about your future and what God is doing right now because you made the decision to take off those old garments and replace them with the garment of praise. I'm in expectation of the shift that God is getting ready to make in you as you are reading this. But I want you to feel the shift that He's getting ready to do in your life, it is impossible for me to feel it for you. This is a shift you have to receive on your own. You have to have your own relationship with God, because I have a relationship with God I can keep my smile. I don't have to give my smile up and neither do you if you want to keep it.

I understand I am a vessel to be used by God, and He chose me to share parts of my testimony with you about what I have gone through and how He allowed me to go through some hard circumstances even when I was on kingdom assignments for his glory. No matter how hard it got , trust this about me, you will hardly ever see me down and even if I fall down i get right back up. Not many will get the pleasure of seeing me down because it's what's on the inside of me that causes me to be a fighter and a fighter will always get back up. I choose to not only just get up, but i do it with a smile. It's not because everything is running on all cylinders, but I recognize that you don't even know half the story or half of the stuff that I had to go through in order to write my story and share it with you. Right now, as you are reading, some of you are going through a situation and you have no idea how to break this thing. Even after all

I have shared so far, you are still sitting right where you are in your own personal Ziklag experience. Just know, this circumstance, these things that's going on in your life are just temporary. Say this with me as you talk to the problem, "You are temporary boo!" God is only allowing you to go throw this set back because he has your comeback in mind! Your bounce back is here now go ahead and celebrate your victory!!!!!!

Conclusion

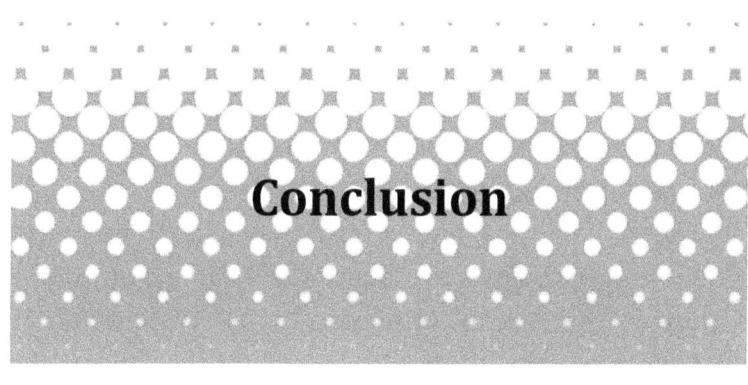

I would like to end this book at the place where I first began, sitting in the middle of the floor in my living room, clinging onto my pillow with tears streaming, shouting, *Really God?* as I sat in the middle of the worst season of my life. As I reflect on that moment, I do so only as a point of closure with all who will read the pages of this book on my mind. I would be remiss to leave you thinking that life will be perfect always, however I reference my tears and I recall the major paradigm shift in my life. Because my reason for writing this book was simply a desire to take you with me as I shifted in my thinking; shifting my attitude towards gratitude and shifted my focus on God. As I remind each of you, in order to move on in your amazing future, you must first shift in your mind.

Reflection is not always about you, but for everyone that you will share your life's testimony with and as Jesus told Peter, "When you are delivered, go and strengthen your brethren." *Luke 22:31-33 (below)*

"Simon, Simon, behold, Satan has demanded permission to sift you like wheat; but I have prayed for

you, that your faith may not fail; and you, when once you have turned again, strengthen your brothers." But he said to Him, *"Lord, with You I am ready to go both to prison and to death!"*[26]

You see we are not alone, as we like Peter and David and many others have a spiritual target on our backs as the enemy attempts to throw fiery darts (accusations, lies, innuendos) we find ourselves trying to dodge these attempts at every turn. However let me remind once again, don't get discouraged in your Ziklag, never give up while you are going through your PROCESS, remember it is only TEMPORARY, you have got to ENCOURAGE yourself, be RESILIENT, always keep your KODAK SMILE as you prepare for your BOUNCE BACK!

26"Luke 22:32 But I have prayed for you, Simon, that your faith ..." 2013. 14 May. 2015 <http://biblehub.com/luke/22-32.htm>

Meet Pastor Orienthia Speakman

Affectionately called by those who know and love her, *Pastor "O"*, Orienthia Speakman has been ministering to the hearts of God's people over 15 years and many refer to her as *"The Keep It Real Preacher"* because of her authentic style mixed with transparency and coupled with a delightful boldness. *Listen up, don't pass the mic to Pastor Orienthia if you don't desire to hear the truth in the message of God's word.* Pastor Orienthia fiery sermons are explosive as well as unforgettable. She is most remembered for her discourse titled, *"There is Power in Your Process".*

As the Founder and CEO of CR8NME Ministry, a mentorship group for woman that focuses on empowering and encouraging sisters through practical biblical teaching to live a balanced and productive Christ centered life.

With a desire to please God and impact the world. she has been an Ordained Minister since 2000 and has earned a degree in Psychology and most recently has become a Certified Transformational Coach. Pastor Orienthia currently serves as Pastor of Christian Education at Bethel Original Freewill Baptist Church in Decatur, GA.

Pastor Orienthia has served in various capacities in ministry, but her passion and personal desire is to educate God's people in order for matured Christians to be developed. She strongly believes that biblical principles must become practical living in order to see transformation in our lives.

She has authored several books: *Really God? A Guide to Bouncing Back When Life Has Thrown You Down* and *Bouncing Back A 40 Day Personal Devotional, Kingdom Bombshells Guide to being Explosive(Compilation).*

Product Page

$12.00

$20.00

Purchase your copy today on Amazon.com or contact author directly via email @cre8nmeministry@yahoo.com for more ordering information.

www.ingramcontent.com/pod-product-compliance
Lightning Source LLC
Chambersburg PA
CBHW071153090426
42736CB00012B/2319